DISCOVER MY WORLD

Forest

Written by Ron Hirschi
Illustrated by Barbara Bash

A BANTAM LITTLE ROOSTER BOOK
NEW YORK · TORONTO · LONDON · SYDNEY · AUCKLAND

FOREST

A Bantam Little Rooster Book / September 1991
Little Rooster is a trademark of Bantam Books, a division of
Bantam Doubleday Dell Publishing Group, Inc.
Library of Congress Cataloging-in-Publication Data
Hirschi, Ron.
    Forest / by Ron Hirschi ; illustrated by Barbara Bash.
        p.   cm. — (Discover my world)
    Summary: By answering questions posed by the text, the reader
must guess the identity of various animals found in the forest.
    ISBN 0-553-07469-5. — ISBN 0-553-35213-X (pbk.)
    1. Forest ecology—Juvenile literature. [1. Forest ecology.
2. Forests and forestry.] I. Bash, Barbara, ill. II. Title.
III. Series: Hirschi, Ron. Discover my world.
QH86.H57 1991
574.5′2642—dc20   90-31813
                                                                          CIP
                                                                          AC
Published simultaneously in the United States and Canada

Bantam Books are published by Bantam Books, a division
of Bantam Doubleday Dell Publishing Group, Inc. Its
trademark, consisting of the words "Bantam Books" and
the portrayal of a rooster, is Registered in U.S. Patent
and Trademark Office and in other countries. Marca
Registrada. Bantam Books, 666 Fifth Avenue, New
York, New York 10103.

PRINTED IN HONG KONG

0 9 8 7 6 5 4 3 2 1

For my special friend, Florian

—R.H.

To Erin

—B.B.

Some time in the night
or early-morning light,
a tiny tree begins to grow.
Who will live with the tree
during its long, long life
by the woodland stream?

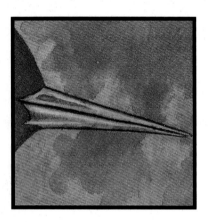

Tap! Tap! Tap!
Tap! Tap! Tap!
Who am I,
hammering for beetles
in the aspen's bark
and building my house
in its soft, white wood?

When the woodpeckers
move out, who will live
in the aspen tree next year?

Who hides with ears alert
while the chickadee sings?

Who hunts on wings
that slice the wind?

And who slithers
through the dew-drenched grass,
slipping past the silent rabbit?

Who am I,
nibbling petals one by one
from flowers growing
in the sun?

Can you guess my name?
Do you see the spots
that dot my back like flowers
in the meadow grass?

Who's that chattering in a branch
high overhead?

Who flies by,
fluttering on the breeze
in search of sweet nectar?
Fly fast. The wind grows strong.

Who am I,
splashing my tail in the sun?
My work never seems to be done.

Who leaps so high
in the beavers' pond?

And who followed the dragonfly
along the path
to this rainbow's pool?
Is it me, or is it you?

Tiny tree seedlings have delicate, new growth. They are often nibbled by rabbits and deer and others. As their branches grow strong, their leaves become tough and not so tasty.

The woodpecker's head and bill are specially adapted for pounding. The woodpecker's tail is also unique. The pointed tip of each tail feather digs into the tree trunk to help the bird hold tight while hammering for dinner.

The wings of a sharp-shinned hawk are specially adapted to life in the forest. Short and rounded, they help the hawk fly between branches as it chases small birds through tangles of trees.

A snake's scales help it to move through the forest. It is no accident that these scales point tailward. Like treads on a running shoe, the snake's layer of scales helps it cling and push forward.

Forest Discoveries

 Chickadees have very small bills, just right for poking into tight places for insects. But chickadee bills aren't strong enough to chip away wood. So, like many other birds, they depend on woodpeckers to build their homes.

 Rabbit whiskers are sensitive to the slightest touch. Like cats, they can use their whiskers to find out whether a small space is wide enough for them to enter.

 An eye stripe on the chipmunk's face helps conceal a blink or a stare. Predators have a harder time seeing which way the chipmunk is heading because the stripe runs the entire length of this small mammal's body.

 A fawn's spots seem to be painted on, and are one of many examples of cryptic coloration in nature. Like a nesting bird's feather color or speckles on an egg, spots help the deer fawn escape the sharp eyes of predators.

 A squirrel chatters and all the forest listens. A warning to others, the voice of the red squirrel is known by deer, small birds, and large predators as well.

 Look closely at a butterfly's wing. No architect or engineer could repeat this delicate pattern. Like pieces of an intricate puzzle, the patterns and colors are formed by thousands of tiny scales. No two butterflies have exactly the same design.

 A swimming beaver uses its wide, flat tail to steer in the water much like a rudder. It also makes a handy prop, helping the beaver to stand steady while it cuts down a tree with its sharp teeth.

 Trout jump with the help of their wide tails and the strong muscles that line their bodies. Their armlike fins also help guide them over small waterfalls and to catch flying insects.